Minibeast Pets
Caterpillars

by Theresa Greenaway

Photography by Chris Fairclough

WAYLAND

Minibeast Pets

Caterpillars   Spiders
Slugs and Snails   Worms

Cover photograph: An emperor moth caterpillar.

All Wayland books encourage
children to read and help them improve their literacy.

 The contents page, page numbers, headings, diagrams and index help locate specific pieces of information.

 The glossary reinforces alphabetic knowledge and extends vocabulary.

 On page 30 you can find out about other books, videos and a CD-ROM dealing with the same subject.

© Copyright 1999 (text) Wayland Publishers Limited
61 Western Road, Hove, East Sussex BN3 1JD

Planned and produced by Discovery Books Limited
Project Editors: Gianna Williams, Kathy DeVico
Project Manager: Joyce Spicer
Illustrated by Stuart Lafford and Stefan Chabluk
Designed by Ian Winton

British Library Cataloguing in Publication Data
Greenaway, Theresa, 1947-
    Caterpillars. – (Minibeast Pets)
    1. Caterpillars – Juvenile literature
    2. Invertebrates as pets – Juvenile literature
    I. Title
    595.7'8139
HARDBACK   ISBN 0 7502 2507 6
PAPERBACK   ISBN 0 7502 2511 4
Printed and bound in the USA

Find Wayland on the Internet at http://www.wayland.co.uk

WARNING
Some hairy caterpillars can cause unpleasant allergic responses, such as itchy rashes. Hairs can detach from the caterpillar and work their way into human skin. Children and adults should avoid touching all hairy caterpillars.

Contents

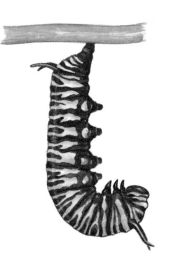

Introducing caterpillars

Caterpillars are the larvae of butterflies and moths. They make ideal pets, and it is great fun to watch them grow and change.

A female butterfly or moth lays its eggs on a plant. When the tiny caterpillars are ready to hatch, they nibble their way out of their eggshells. Then they use their sharp jaws to eat plant leaves.

◄ One day this caterpillar will turn into a beautiful swallowtail butterfly.

It takes from a few weeks to several months for a caterpillar to grow to its full size. It then becomes a pupa. This is the halfway stage between a caterpillar and a moth or butterfly.

Caterpillars have long, tube-shaped bodies. Below their mouths are tiny silk glands. Just behind a caterpillar's head are three pairs of tiny true legs. Towards their back end there are usually ten stumpy legs called prolegs.

prolegs

body segments

head

spiracles
Allow air in and out of the body

Inside the pupa, the caterpillar changes into an adult insect, with wings. If you take good care of your caterpillar, you will be able to enjoy all these stages.

true legs

Finding caterpillars

You can search for caterpillars anywhere that plants grow.

Look carefully at the leaves of flowers, vegetables and weeds.

Good places to look are on nettles, cabbages, fruit trees, oak trees and brambles.

Caterpillars try to hide from hungry birds, so finding them can take a while. Many kinds are camouflaged to blend in with their surroundings.

◄ If you look closely, you can see a looper caterpillar on this branch. It is camouflaged to look just like a small brown twig.

6

Some caterpillars only come out at night,
when most birds are asleep.

Silky homes

Tent caterpillars use their silk glands to make themselves a silk tent. If you look in a wild cherry tree, you may find hundreds of tiny caterpillars sharing one tent.

Other kinds of caterpillars roll leaves around themselves. Then they wrap the leaves with silk to make tubes, which they live in.

Caterpillar collecting

Caterpillars are quite soft and can be damaged easily, so handle them very gently. You can move caterpillars by lifting them with a small, soft paintbrush.

Another way is to cut and collect leaves or twigs that have caterpillars on them. If you do this, you don't have to disturb the caterpillars at all.

Find as many different caterpillars as you can. Put the different kinds into separate jars or plastic containers, adding fresh leaves from each caterpillar's own food plant.

Make sure the containers all have lids with air holes.

Stick a label on each container, saying where and when you found the caterpillars inside, and what they were eating.

Hairy warning

Some kinds of caterpillars shed hairs that can cause rashes, so try not to touch them. This brown-tailed moth caterpillar is very pretty, but its hairs will give you an itchy rash if they get stuck in your skin.

Identifying caterpillars

When you have collected some caterpillars, it is time to identify them. This is not always easy, even for experts. Some are common garden pests, while others are rare.

A book with pictures of caterpillars may help you find out what they are.

If you know the name of the plant a caterpillar is eating, it may help you identify the caterpillar.

If you cannot identify your new pets, write a description, or draw them in your notebook.

▶ This large white butterfly caterpillar likes to eat the leaves of cabbages.

If you keep the caterpillars until they pupate and turn into butterflies or moths, it will be much easier to identify them.

Next time you come across these caterpillars, you will know exactly what they are.

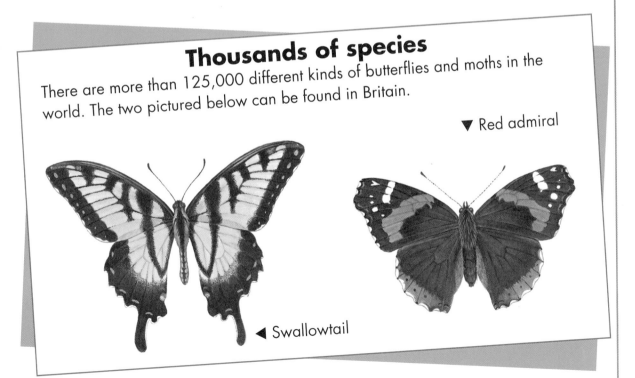

Thousands of species

There are more than 125,000 different kinds of butterflies and moths in the world. The two pictured below can be found in Britain.

▼ Red admiral

◀ Swallowtail

Homes for caterpillars

Your caterpillars will need a good home while you are keeping them. A small plastic box or glass jar, with air holes in its lid, is fine for little caterpillars. As well as letting in air, the holes stop the container becoming too damp inside.

Line the container with paper towels.

Underground homes

Some caterpillars, such as this tomato hornworm moth larva, need soil to burrow into when they are ready to pupate. If you keep any kind of burrowing caterpillars, you will need to add a layer of soil to their home.

lid

Put fresh leaves on the paper towels, and carefully move the little caterpillars onto the leaves with a soft paintbrush.

paper towel　　**fresh leaves**

If you want to keep caterpillars until they change into moths and butterflies, they will need a larger home.

When the caterpillars are bigger, move them to a shoebox or larger plastic container covered with netting or wire mesh.

Caring for caterpillars

Caterpillars don't need much looking after, but you must give them plenty of fresh food. They also need fresh air, and the right amount of moisture.

Try to keep caterpillars in conditions as near as possible to those where they were found.

Breathing bodies

Caterpillars take in air through tiny holes, called spiracles, along their sides.

Caterpillars will die if they are too wet or too dry. Don't put them in full sunshine, or next to a heater, or anywhere cold and damp.

Unless you clean the caterpillars' homes, mould will grow that could kill your minibeast pets.

Be sure to remove all wilted leaves, any caterpillars that die, and as many of the caterpillars' droppings as possible.

Feeding caterpillars

Some caterpillars are very picky about what they eat. They will only eat one kind of leaf. Others are not nearly so fussy.

It is important to identify what caterpillars are eating when you find them.

▲ Woolly bear caterpillars eat many different kinds of leaves.

You may need to find more plants of the same kind, so that you do not run out of leaves.

You can look in a caterpillar guide to see if there is something else they will eat. Any new leaves must be fed to them gradually, before you have run out of the caterpillars' usual food.

Poisonous prey

Caterpillars of the monarch butterfly eat poisonous milkweed leaves. The caterpillar is not affected by the poison, which it stores in its skin. The colourful markings of the caterpillar warn birds that they will be sick if they eat it.

Tiny caterpillars need young, delicate leaves. As they grow, the caterpillars' jaws get stronger, and they can chew much tougher leaves. But caterpillars will not eat wilted or dying leaves.

Watching caterpillars

You can learn a lot about your pets by watching them through a magnifying glass. You will soon see that caterpillars are simply eating machines! Can you see the caterpillars' jaws? Do they all bite and chew in the same way?

Watch how caterpillars move. On each of a caterpillar's prolegs there are tiny hooks. These grip onto the surface of leaves and twigs so that the caterpillar does not fall off.

The front legs are used mostly to guide the caterpillar and to hold leaves for eating.

▼ This tiger moth caterpillar is using its prolegs to grip tightly onto a branch.

Moving house

The bagworm caterpillar spins a silk case around itself, sticking in tiny pieces of plants for extra protection. It moves around with the bag sticking up behind it. The bag will become its cocoon.

As a caterpillar grows, its skin becomes too tight. The caterpillar moults to get rid of its outgrown skin. If your caterpillar stops moving around and eating, it may just be too big for its skin.

▼ Here you can see a caterpillar wriggling out of its old, tight skin. The new skin underneath is looser.

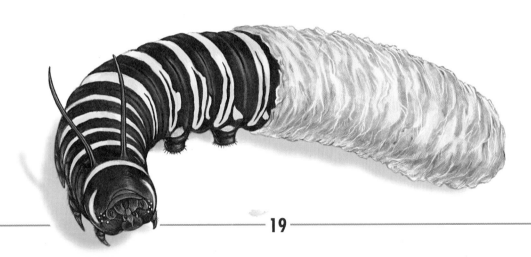

Growing up

When it is fully grown, a caterpillar pupates.

The pupa of a butterfly or moth is often called a chrysalis.

▶ Many moth caterpillars spin a cocoon of silk to protect their chrysalis.

Pupa preparations

You may see your caterpillar attach itself to a leaf or twig. Its skin rolls back to show the pupa underneath. The pupa case hardens and protects the insect while it changes into an adult.

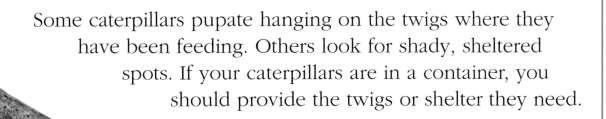

Some caterpillars pupate hanging on the twigs where they have been feeding. Others look for shady, sheltered spots. If your caterpillars are in a container, you should provide the twigs or shelter they need.

Caterpillars that pupate underground may move around in the dirt on the bottom of their container for several days before they begin.

Once the caterpillar has found a safe place to pupate, its skin starts to split. This time, underneath the old skin is a pupa case.

Inside the chrysalis, the wingless caterpillar changes into the winged, adult insect. Then the pupa case splits, and the adult insect struggles out.

▲ When its wings have dried, this new butterfly will be able to fly.

When winter comes

In the winter it is much too cold for caterpillars to move around. Many plants lose all their leaves, and so there is no food. How will your pets get through the winter?

▼ The giant silkworm caterpillar will spend the winter as a pupa in its cocoon.

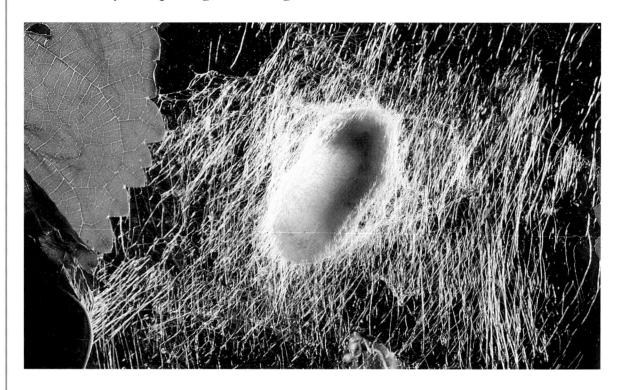

Many caterpillars never see winter. Some hatch in the spring and turn into adult insects by autumn. Others are fully grown caterpillars by autumn, and pass the winter months as pupae.

Check your caterpillar guide to see what your pets will do in the winter.

You may have caterpillars that will survive by hibernating. Some hide away on their food plant. Others crawl underground and stay there until the weather warms up. While they are hibernating, caterpillars do not move or eat.

Other kinds of butterfly migrate. As soon as autumn arrives, they fly to warmer places.

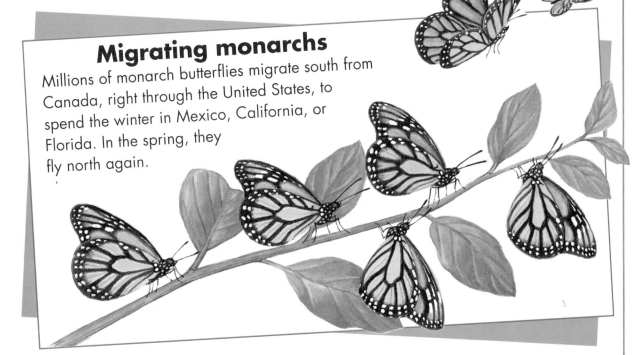

Migrating monarchs

Millions of monarch butterflies migrate south from Canada, right through the United States, to spend the winter in Mexico, California, or Florida. In the spring, they fly north again.

Keeping a record

You can have a lot of fun studying caterpillars. It is a good idea to keep a scrapbook and write down everything you learn about your pets.

Paste in any pictures or articles that you find in magazines.

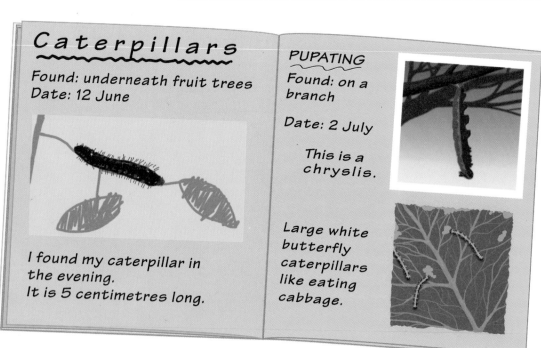

Caterpillars

Found: underneath fruit trees
Date: 12 June

I found my caterpillar in the evening.
It is 5 centimetres long.

PUPATING
Found: on a branch

Date: 2 July

This is a chryslis.

Large white butterfly caterpillars like eating cabbage.

Compare the life cycle of one kind of caterpillar with another. Make a note of what they eat, what they look like, and how they change as they grow larger.

Write down the date that they pupate. Describe what the chrysalises look like, and if they change colour just before hatching.

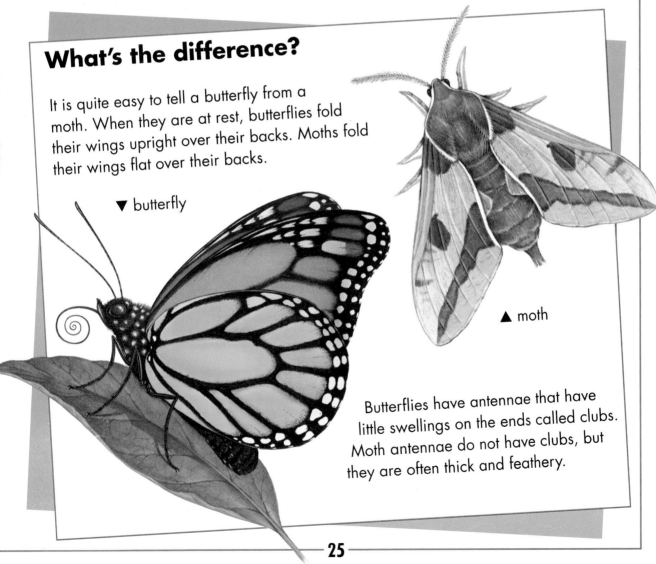

What's the difference?

It is quite easy to tell a butterfly from a moth. When they are at rest, butterflies fold their wings upright over their backs. Moths fold their wings flat over their backs.

▼ butterfly

▲ moth

Butterflies have antennae that have little swellings on the ends called clubs. Moth antennae do not have clubs, but they are often thick and feathery.

Letting them go

You may want to release your caterpillars before they pupate. If you decide to let them go, make sure you put them back onto their food plant.

You can keep your pets until they turn into butterflies or moths. If you are lucky, you will see the adult insect crawl out of its chrysalis. Wait until its wings are dry and it is ready to fly before letting it go.

Butterflies can be released during the day. But remember that many moths fly only in the dark.

Your pets will fly away to feed. Butterflies and moths feed on nectar, a liquid they find in flowers.

World's biggest butterfly
This is the Queen Alexandra's birdwing butterfly from Papua New Guinea. The female has a wingspan of 15 to 28 cm.

▼ A comma butterfly feeding on the sugary nectar of a fleabane flower.

Releasing your very own butterflies or moths that you have raised from tiny caterpillars is a wonderful thing to do. If you try to keep them in cages, they will damage their lovely wings by trying to escape.

Caterpillar facts

Caterpillars that can defend themselves are usually brightly coloured. They may have an unpleasant taste or smell, or have hairs that can sting.

▲ Cinnebar moth caterpillar

▼ Monarch butterfly caterpillar

These two caterpillars have a nasty taste.

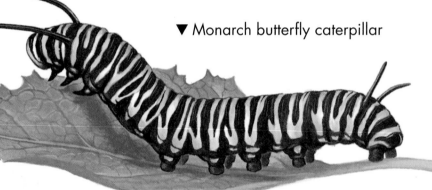

Their bright markings warn predators to leave them alone. This means they do not have to hide.

Asian silkworm caterpillars spin large cocoons. Over 4,000 years ago, people in China discovered how to turn these into silk cloth. All the silk made today still comes from these silkworms.

◀ Swallowtail butterfly caterpillar

When they are young and small, swallowtail butterfly caterpillars disguise themselves as bird droppings. This means they can sit on leaves in safety, because birds will not eat each other's droppings!

Not all caterpillars eat leaves. Clothes moth caterpillars eat wool or velvet.

▼ The caterpillar of the large blue butterfly being carried by ants.

The caterpillars of the European large blue butterfly are sometimes captured by ants and carried into the ants' nest. These caterpillars produce a sugary liquid that the ants like to eat.

Finding out more

BOOKS

Explorers: Butterflies and Moths by John Feltwell (Dorling Kindersley, 1998)

From Caterpillar to Butterfly by Gerald Legg (Watts, 1997)

My Best Book of Creepy Crawlies by Claire Llewellyn (Kingfisher, 1998)

Wings, Stings and Wriggly Things: *Minibeasts* by M. Jenkins (Walker, 1996)

CD-ROM

Insects: Little Creatures in a Big World (Ransom Publishing, 1997)

VIDEOS

Amazing Animals: Creepy Crawly Animals (Dorling Kindersley, 1999)

Amazing Animals: Minibeasts (Dorling Kindersley, 1996)

Eyewitness: Butterfly and Moth (Dorling Kindersley, 1996)

FURTHER INFORMATION

CLEAPPS School Science Service will be able to help with any aspect of keeping minibeasts.   Tel: 01895 251496

SCIENCE
Observing minibeasts
Animal classification /
  variation
Animal habitats
Life cycles
Life processes
Moving and growing
Food chains / nutrition
Animal adaptations
Animal behaviour
Use of magnifying
  glass

ENGLISH
Following instructions
Recording
  observations
Using glossaries
Extending scientific
  vocabulary
Research skills

ART, DESIGN & TECHNOLOGY
Close observation:
  drawings of
  minibeasts
Investigating
  camouflage / mimicry
Designing and making
  (scrapbooks,
  containers for
  minibeasts)

Minibeast Pets TOPIC WEB

MATHS
Measuring skills
Collecting and
  recording data

GEOGRAPHY
The seasons
Weather and climate

PHSE
Caring for living things
Showing respect
Taking responsibility

Glossary

antennae The two feelers on the head of an insect which are sensitive to touch and smell.

camouflage The colouring and patterns on an animal's body that help it to blend in with its surroundings, and hide it from predators.

chrysalis Another name for the pupa of a moth or butterfly.

cocoon A case of silk spun by a caterpillar.

hibernate To spend the winter resting in a sheltered place.

identify To find out the name of something.

larva (plural **larvae**) The wingless, often wormlike form of a newly-hatched insect.

migrate To travel a long distance to spend part of each year in a different climate.

moult To get rid of the tough outer skin.

predator An animal that hunts and kills another animal for food.

prolegs The stumpy back legs of caterpillars.

pupa (plural **pupae**) The stage in the life cycle of some insects when the larva changes into an adult with wings.

pupate When the larvae of some groups of insects stay still inside a case while turning into an adult.

silk glands Tiny organs that squeeze out droplets of liquid. The caterpillar pulls these into threads of silk.

spiracles Breathing holes along each side of a caterpillar's body.

true legs Three pairs of jointed legs at the front end of a caterpillar.

Index

The publishers would like to thank the following for their permission to reproduce photographs:
cover Kim Taylor/Bruce Coleman, 4 Bruce Coleman, 6 Robert A. Lubeck/Oxford Scientific Films, 7 Jack Dermid/
Bruce Coleman, 9 G.E. Hyde/Frank Lane Picture Agency, 11 Hans Reinhard/Bruce Coleman, 12 Donald Specker/Oxford
Scientific Films, 14 Silvestris/Frank Lane Picture Agency, 16 Alvin E. Staffan/Oxford Scientific Films, 17 David
Wrigglesworth/Oxford Scientific Films, 18 J. Brackenbury/Bruce Coleman, 19 Peter Davey/Bruce Coleman,
20 G. E Hyde/Frank Lane Picture Agency, 21 & 22 Kim Taylor/Bruce Coleman,
27 Larry Crowhurst/Oxford Scientific Films, 29 Marie Read/Bruce Coleman